The Bad-News Report Card

Nancy
Poydar

Holiday House / New York

Text and illustrations copyright © 2006 by Nancy Poydar
All Rights Reserved
Manufactured in China
www.holidayhouse.com
The text typeface is Agenda.
The artwork was created with gouache and pencil.
First Edition
1 3 5 7 9 10 8 6 4 2

Library of Congress Cataloging-in-Publication Data

Poydar, Nancy.
The bad-news report card / by Nancy Poydar. — 1st ed.
p. cm.

Summary: Fearing that her report card will not contain good news,
Isabel tries to devise a way to hide it from her parents.

ISBN-13: 978-0-8234-1992-0 (hardcover)
ISBN-10: 0-8234-1992-4 (hardcover)

[1. Report cards—Fiction. 2. Schools—Fiction.]   I. Title.

PZ7.P8846Bad 2006
[E]—dc22   2005021801

Designed by Yvette Lenhart

For Kate Briggs — A+

Isabel Bloom's class was going to get report cards soon. Isabel knew because Ms. Bean was explaining the report card words.

Isabel was absolutely sure her report card would be *excellent*. She imagined showing it to her family. They would shout, "Good news!"

That night Isabel made a report
card for her cat, Badbreath.

The next day Isabel told Adam, "I'm getting an *excellent* report card because I work very hard. I'm going to be a teacher like Ms. Bean. I already know how to *make* report cards."

"Isabel!" said Ms. Bean. "You're whispering, not *listening*."

Uh-oh, thought Isabel. She worried about not *listening* and forgot to put her name on her paper.

"I have a paper with no name on it," said Ms. Bean. "Remember, it doesn't count if I don't know whose it is."

"Isabel *needs improvement*," whispered Adam.

Isabel spied the pile of papers on Ms. Bean's desk. I'll help Ms. Bean know whose paper it is, she thought. She slipped her paper out of the pile and had her pencil ready.

"Isabel Bloom!" called Ms. Bean.

"You look pink," said Adam.

Isabel stuck out her tongue at Adam.

"Isabel!" said Ms. Bean.

"Very pink," said Adam.

At the end of the day, Ms. Bean handed out report cards.

On the bus Isabel stared at her report card.
It was sealed. Her parents would have to sign it.
It absolutely had to be a bad-news report card.

No, Isabel loved her mama and papa too much to give them news like this. She had a *problem to solve*. The bad-news report card disappeared behind the seat on the bus and got itself absolutely stuck.

"Isabel, you look pink. Do you feel all right?" asked her mother.

"My report card disappeared," mumbled Isabel, and she turned pinker. "Would you like to see Badbreath's report card?"

"I'll write a note to Ms. Bean," said Isabel's papa.

On the way to school, Isabel's papa's note disappeared behind the seat on the bus and got itself absolutely stuck.

"You look pink," said Adam.

At school, Mr. Tripp, the principal, made an announcement. "Boys and girls, please remember to bring back your signed report cards."

At home, Isabel's papa and mama wanted to know why Ms. Bean didn't reply to the note.

Isabel was miserable.

On the way to school, Adam said, "I got one *excellent* and two *good*s! How was your report card?"

Isabel didn't know what to say. But she did know she still had a *problem,* and it was time to *solve* it for good!

She reached behind the seat to get her report card and her papa's note. She would give the note to Ms. Bean. She would show the report card to her parents.

But Isabel's report card wasn't stuck behind the seat or under it or anywhere else on the bus. Neither was her papa's note!

Isabel imagined the worst!

"Mr. Tripp is waiting for us," said Ms. Bean at the doorway.

Isabel was pink. She couldn't think. She wanted to disappear like her report card.

"Isabel, your bus driver found your report card and this note stuck behind the seat," said Mr. Tripp. Then Mr. Tripp gave the note to Ms. Bean and showed the report card to Isabel.

"This is not news you want to lose!" he said.

All day, Isabel couldn't wait to bring her report card home!

"Mama, Papa, I've got news!"
"Good news!" shouted her mama.
"Good news!" shouted her papa.
Even Badbreath knew the news was good.

REPORT CARD
Isabel Bloom

Arithmetic—Good
Reading—Good
Writing—Good
Science—Good
Social Studies—Good
Listening—Good
Problem Solving—Good
Imagination—Excellent

Isabel has an active imagination
and learns from her mistakes. It is
a pleasure to watch her grow.

Nancy Bean